Quilt Design Masters

Luanne Seymour Cohen

Dale Seymour Publications®

This book is dedicated to my mother who taught me
to love sewing and to my father who taught me that
math can be beautiful.

Project Editor: Joan Gideon
Production: Leanne Collins
Text and Cover Design: Luanne Seymour Cohen

Published by Dale Seymour Publications®, an imprint of the
Alternative Publishing Group of Addison-Wesley Publishing
Company.

Order Number DS21401
ISBN 0-86651-941-6

1 2 3 4 5 6 7 8 9 10-ML-99 98 97 96 95

DALE
SEYMOUR
PUBLICATIONS®
P.O. BOX 10888
PALO ALTO, CA 94303

This book is printed
on recycled paper.

Contents

Contents

Whether they know it or not, quilters have been practicing geometric principles for centuries. Since straight seams are easier to sew than curved ones, the grid naturally evolved as the basis for their designs. By placing simple geometric shapes in various configurations along grid lines, quilters have created countless variations of colorful geometric patterns. Now students can explore these same geometric principles while enjoying the fun of creating their own quilt designs.

Quilt Design Masters is a resource for students, teachers, quilters, and anyone else interested in experimenting with traditional patchwork quilt patterns. It contains grids for reproducing these patterns or creating original designs, an index of quilt patches, and a selection of patchwork patterns.

The first section includes basic grids and special grids for the four most common quilt patterns—four patch, five patch, seven patch, or nine patch. (A patch is a square divided by a grid to allow easy designing and piecing.) The bold lines on the full-page grids for designing variations of these four basic tiling patterns designate the patches. The lighter lines within each patch indicate the type of patch—for example, the four-patch grid evenly divides by four.

The second section, the index of quilt patches, provides a visual reference of nearly 300 traditional patch or block designs. When a quilt block has several different names, I have used the name that is most familiar, or occasionally the easiest to remember or the most interesting. The number under the block indicates the patch grid. The blocks incorporated in patchwork patterns in this book are marked with an asterisk. The others are included for inspiration when creating your own patterns.

A final two sections on patchwork patterns will help students experiment with color and design. These pages illustrate how patchwork patterns have been created from the single block shown at the top of the page. In the sixteen classic patterns in section three, the block is simply repeated horizontally or vertically—by translating, or sliding it. The last section contains some patterns where the block has been rotated 90°. In others, the block has been reflected or even staggered.

The many different pattern variations that can be made from one block can be further varied using different colors and textures. An excellent example of the versatility of a single block design is the poster *Patterns Within Patterns,* reproduced on the cover of this book.

Quilt Design Masters is an excellent classroom resource. Exploring the blocks and patchwork patterns will give students a hands-on understanding of geometric relationships, such as, rotation and reflection. Experimenting with color will help them see shapes and combinations of shapes. You may want your students, individually or in small groups, to design and create paper quilts. Begin by having them explore some of the patterns in this book.

■ Have students color patchwork designs. Tell them they need not change colors at each line. By making adjacent shapes the same color, they can begin to understand how combining shapes creates other shapes—for example, two red triangles can make one red square.

■ Another interesting way to explore patterns is to first have students color one of the patchwork patterns. Then have them cut the pattern into blocks and rearrange them.

After exploring several quilt patterns, trying different color combinations and experimenting with rotation and reflection, students are ready to make a paper quilt.

■ Students may choose one of the block patterns from the final section of this book, or they may prefer to create their own designs. In either case, students should create their basic pattern blocks on a geometric grid. Though they may use the book patterns for ideas, ask them to create the block on a basic grid.

■ Tell students they may use any combination of colors or designs on the basic block, but remind them that it should create an interesting pattern when the blocks are combined.

■ Once they have made at least sixteen copies of their colored blocks, tell them to experiment with the layout before they finally glue the blocks in place. Ask them to explain how the blocks have been combined—using translation (slide) symmetry, reflective (flip) symmetry, or rotational (turn) symmetry.

■ Students can use scraps of cloth to make their quilts look more realistic. Show them how to pin a photocopy of the master pattern to the fabric to guide cutting. Then have them glue (glue sticks work well) the fabric shapes to a master page—one that contains an outline of the pattern. Point out that this is how many quilt makers explore color for their quilts.

■ Other suggested materials for making quilts are wrapping paper, wall paper, or photocopies of fabric. Make sure to include a wide variety of patterns in a range of light to dark tones and delicate to bold designs. Old fabric catalogs and wallpaper books are good sources for these materials

I hope you enjoy exploring these patterns and creating quilt designs of your own.

1

Grids

Eighth-Inch Grid—Dotted

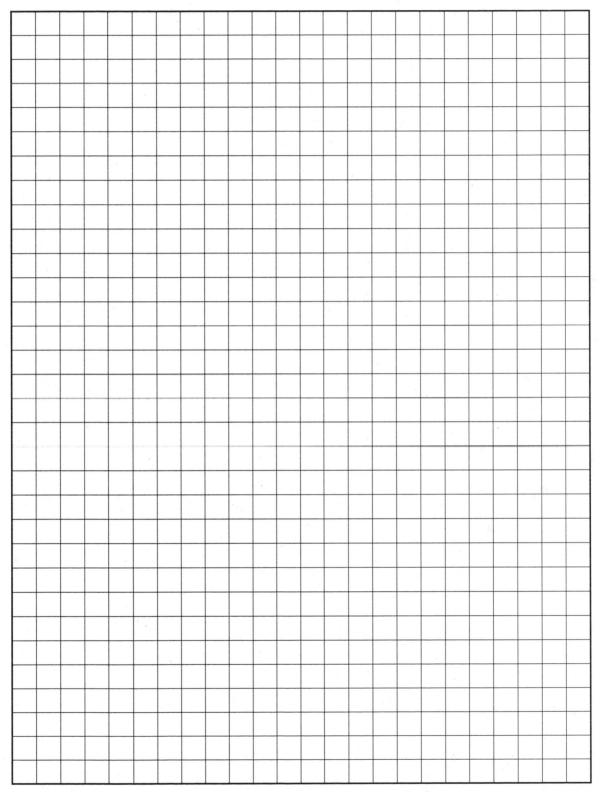

Quarter-Inch Grid—Dotted

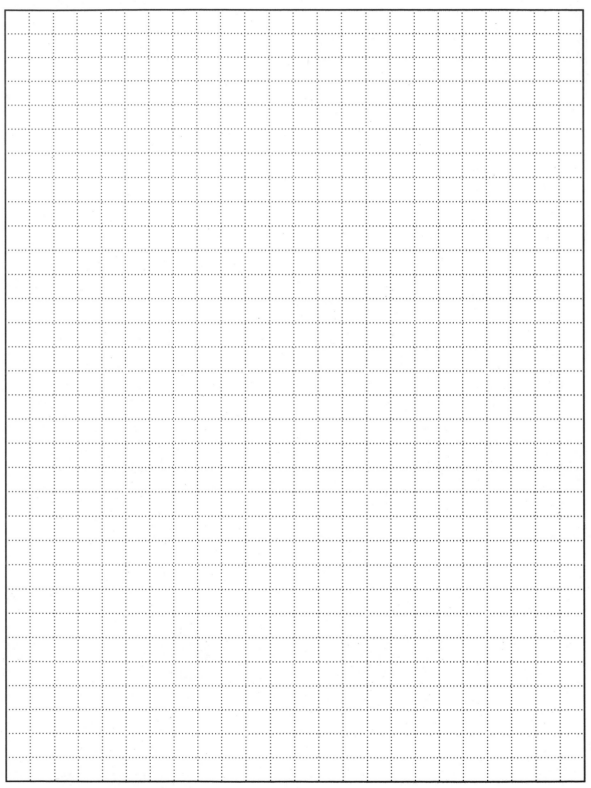

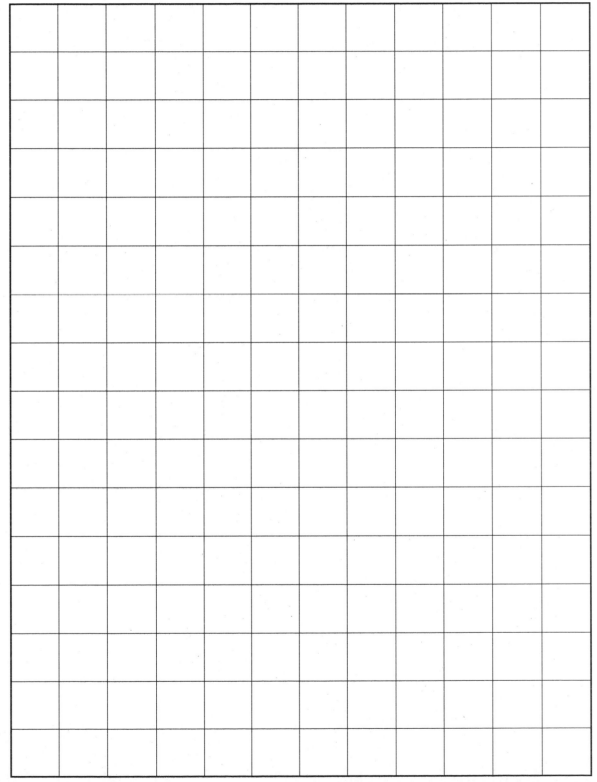

Half-Inch Grid—Dotted

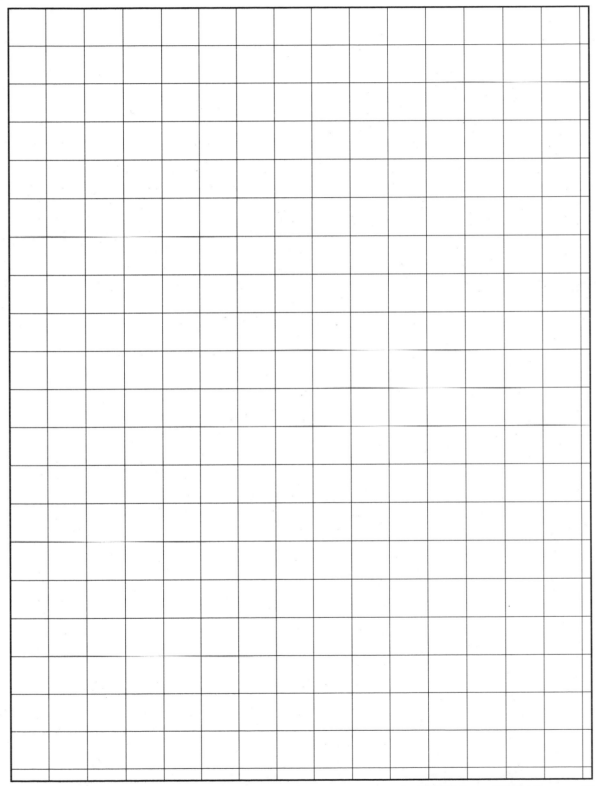

Centimeter Grid—Dotted

Hexagonal Grid—Dotted

Block Masters

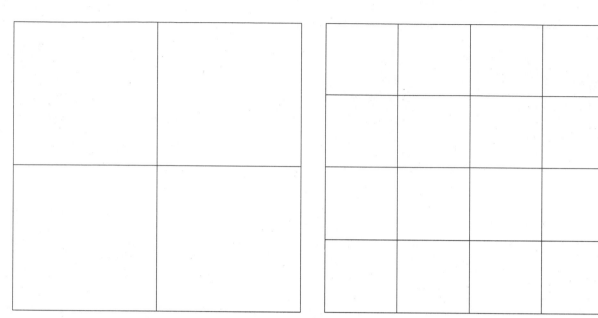

4 patch—4 squares

4 patch—16 squares

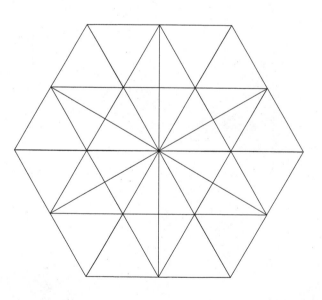

4 patch—64 squares

6-pointed star

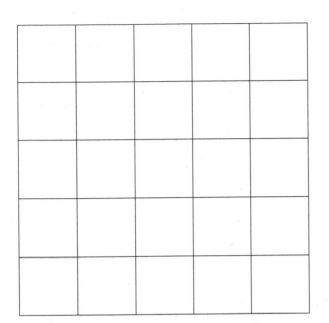

5 patch—25 square

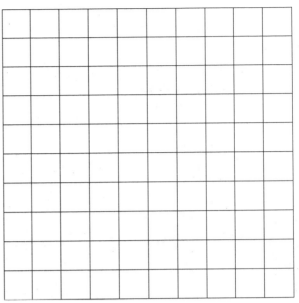

5 patch—100 square

7 patch—49 square

7 patch—196 square

15

Block Masters

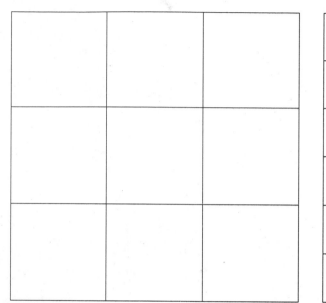

9 patch—9 square

9 patch—81 square

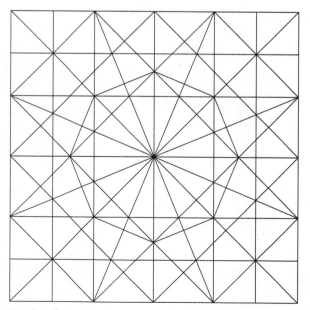

8-pointed star

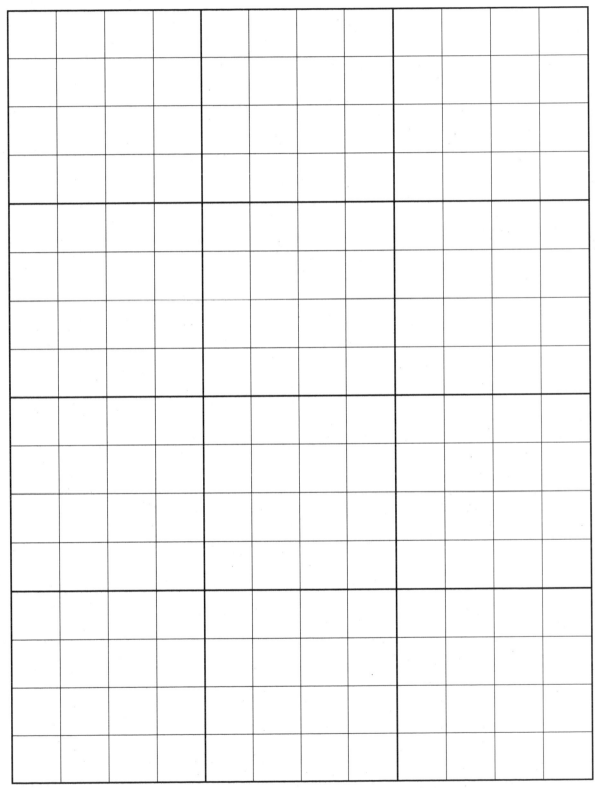

17

Five Patch

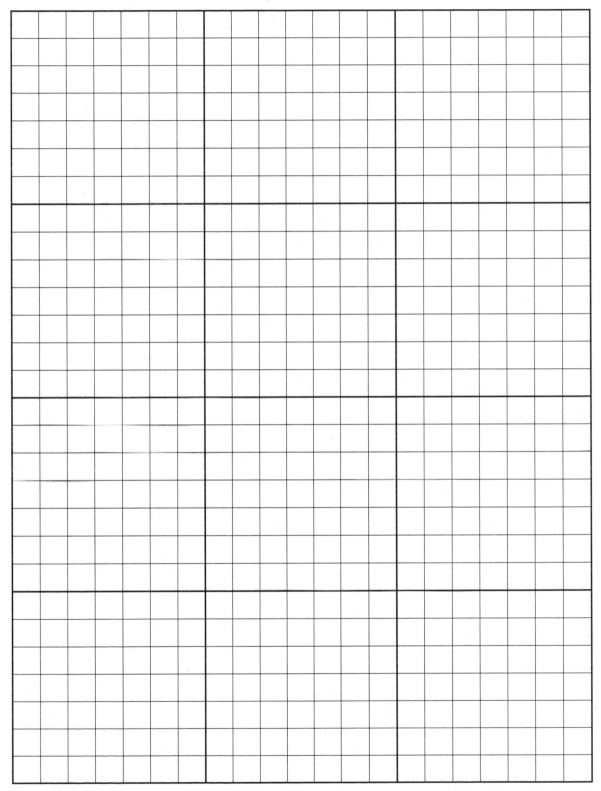

Nine Patch

2
Visual Index

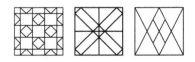

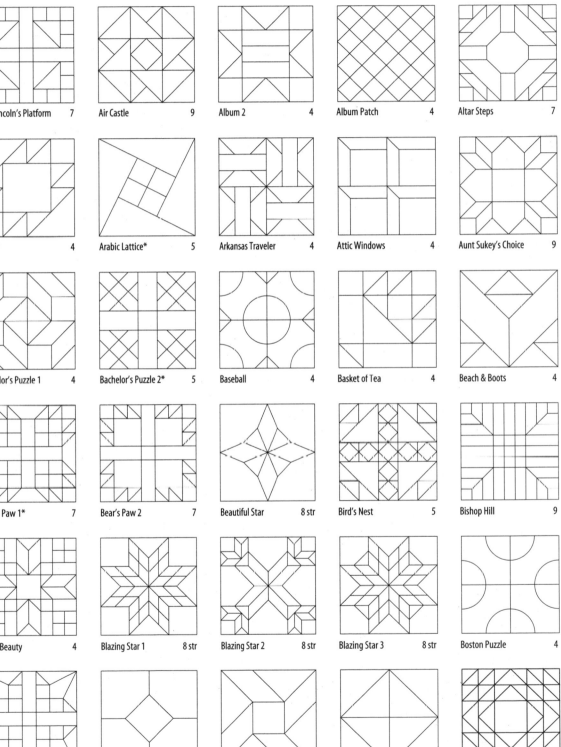

Abe Lincoln's Platform 7	Air Castle 9	Album 2 4	Album Patch 4	Altar Steps 7
Anvil* 4	Arabic Lattice* 5	Arkansas Traveler 4	Attic Windows 4	Aunt Sukey's Choice 9
Bachelor's Puzzle 1 4	Bachelor's Puzzle 2* 5	Baseball 4	Basket of Tea 4	Beach & Boots 4
Bear's Paw 1* 7	Bear's Paw 2 7	Beautiful Star 8 str	Bird's Nest 5	Bishop Hill 9
Black Beauty 4	Blazing Star 1 8 str	Blazing Star 2 8 str	Blazing Star 3 8 str	Boston Puzzle 4
Bouquet 7	Bow Tie 4	Box Quilt* 9	Broken Dishes 4	Broken Windows 9

Visual Index

(number at right indicates the patch grid, asterisk indicates design is elsewhere in this book)

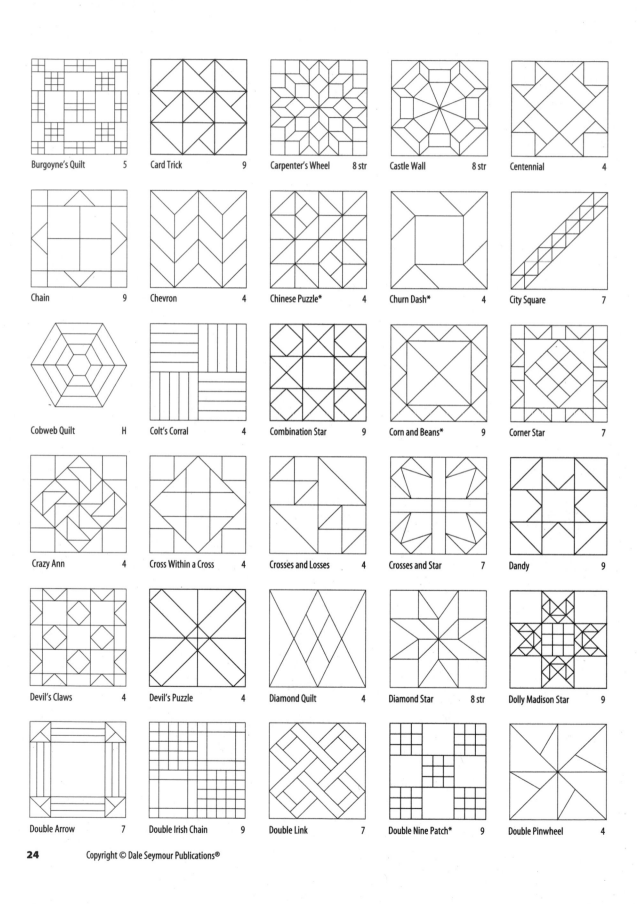

Burgoyne's Quilt 5	Card Trick 9	Carpenter's Wheel 8 str	Castle Wall 8 str	Centennial 4
Chain 9	Chevron 4	Chinese Puzzle* 4	Churn Dash* 4	City Square 7
Cobweb Quilt H	Colt's Corral 4	Combination Star 9	Corn and Beans* 9	Corner Star 7
Crazy Ann 4	Cross Within a Cross 4	Crosses and Losses 4	Crosses and Star 7	Dandy 9
Devil's Claws 4	Devil's Puzzle 4	Diamond Quilt 4	Diamond Star 8 str	Dolly Madison Star 9
Double Arrow 7	Double Irish Chain 9	Double Link 7	Double Nine Patch* 9	Double Pinwheel 4

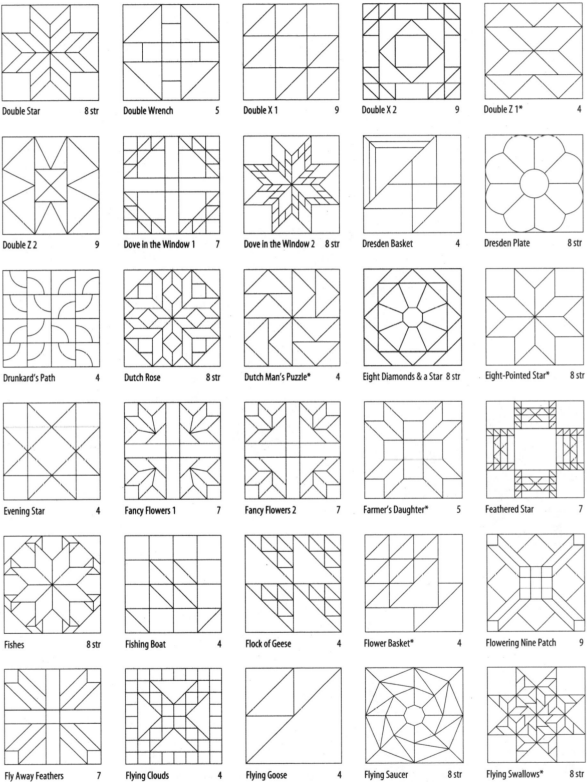

Double Star 8 str	Double Wrench 5	Double X 1 9	Double X 2 9	Double Z 1* 4
Double Z 2 9	Dove in the Window 1 7	Dove in the Window 2 8 str	Dresden Basket 4	Dresden Plate 8 str
Drunkard's Path 4	Dutch Rose 8 str	Dutch Man's Puzzle* 4	Eight Diamonds & a Star 8 str	Eight-Pointed Star* 8 str
Evening Star 4	Fancy Flowers 1 7	Fancy Flowers 2 7	Farmer's Daughter* 5	Feathered Star 7
Fishes 8 str	Fishing Boat 4	Flock of Geese 4	Flower Basket* 4	Flowering Nine Patch 9
Fly Away Feathers 7	Flying Clouds 4	Flying Goose 4	Flying Saucer 8 str	Flying Swallows* 8 str

Visual Index
(number at right indicates the patch grid, asterisk indicates design is elsewhere in this book)

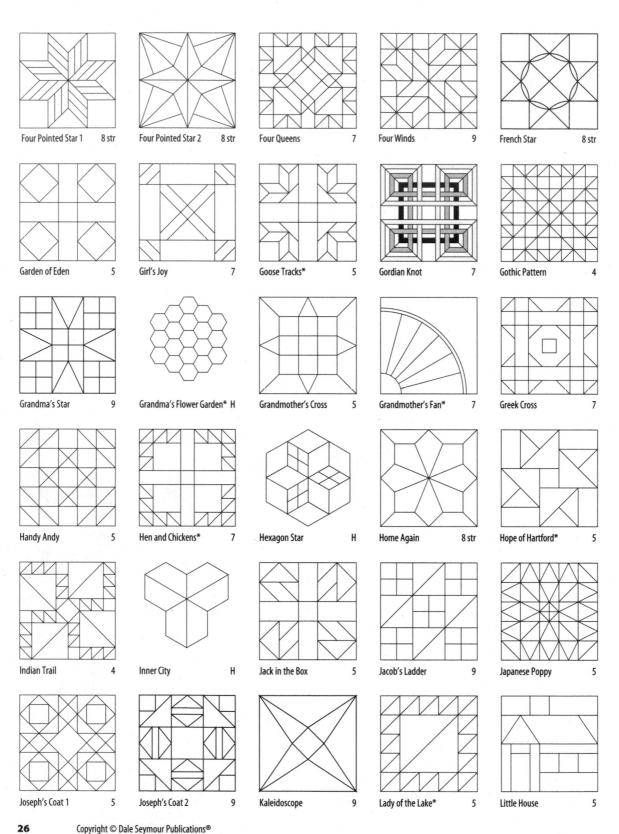

Four Pointed Star 1 8 str	Four Pointed Star 2 8 str	Four Queens 7	Four Winds 9	French Star 8 str
Garden of Eden 5	Girl's Joy 7	Goose Tracks* 5	Gordian Knot 7	Gothic Pattern 4
Grandma's Star 9	Grandma's Flower Garden* H	Grandmother's Cross 5	Grandmother's Fan* 7	Greek Cross 7
Handy Andy 5	Hen and Chickens* 7	Hexagon Star H	Home Again 8 str	Hope of Hartford* 5
Indian Trail 4	Inner City H	Jack in the Box 5	Jacob's Ladder 9	Japanese Poppy 5
Joseph's Coat 1 5	Joseph's Coat 2 9	Kaleidoscope 9	Lady of the Lake* 5	Little House 5

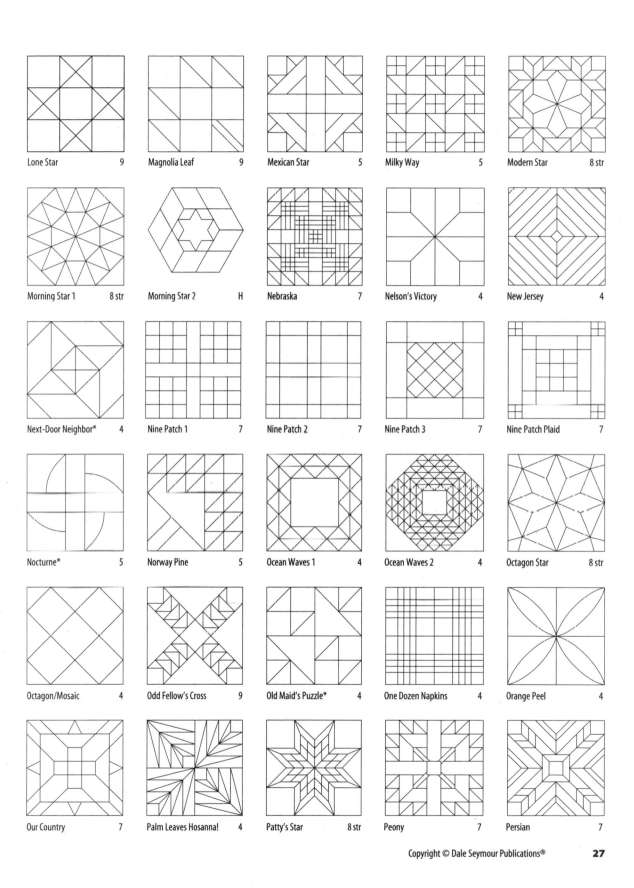

Lone Star — 9	Magnolia Leaf — 9	Mexican Star — 5
Milky Way — 5	Modern Star — 8 str	
Morning Star 1 — 8 str	Morning Star 2 — H	Nebraska — 7
Nelson's Victory — 4	New Jersey — 4	
Next-Door Neighbor* — 4	Nine Patch 1 — 7	Nine Patch 2 — 7
Nine Patch 3 — 7	Nine Patch Plaid — 7	
Nocturne* — 5	Norway Pine — 5	Ocean Waves 1 — 4
Ocean Waves 2 — 4	Octagon Star — 8 str	
Octagon/Mosaic — 4	Odd Fellow's Cross — 9	Old Maid's Puzzle* — 4
One Dozen Napkins — 4	Orange Peel — 4	
Our Country — 7	Palm Leaves Hosanna! — 4	Patty's Star — 8 str
Peony — 7	Persian — 7	

Visual Index
(number at right indicates the patch grid, asterisk indicates design is elsewhere in this book)

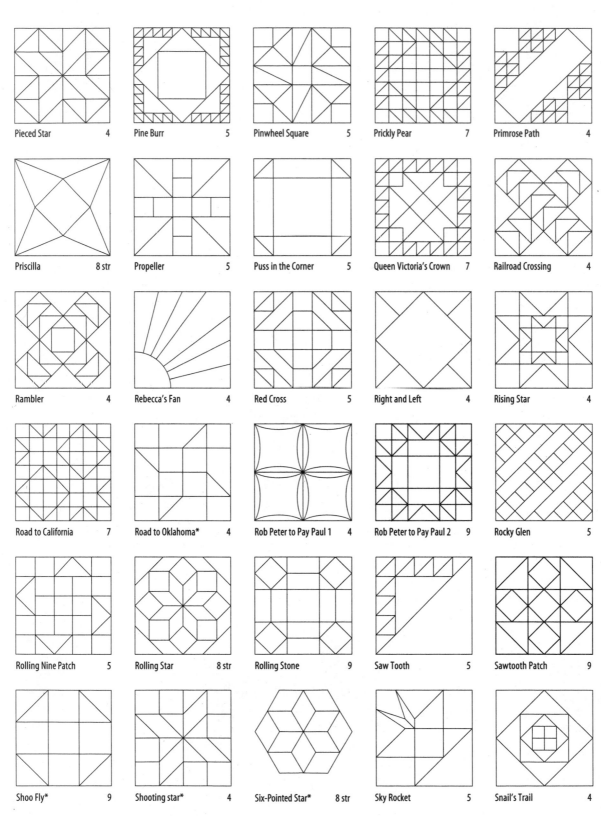

Pieced Star 4	Pine Burr 5	Pinwheel Square 5	Prickly Pear 7	Primrose Path 4
Priscilla 8 str	Propeller 5	Puss in the Corner 5	Queen Victoria's Crown 7	Railroad Crossing 4
Rambler 4	Rebecca's Fan 4	Red Cross 5	Right and Left 4	Rising Star 4
Road to California 7	Road to Oklahoma* 4	Rob Peter to Pay Paul 1 4	Rob Peter to Pay Paul 2 9	Rocky Glen 5
Rolling Nine Patch 5	Rolling Star 8 str	Rolling Stone 9	Saw Tooth 5	Sawtooth Patch 9
Shoo Fly* 9	Shooting star* 4	Six-Pointed Star* 8 str	Sky Rocket 5	Snail's Trail 4

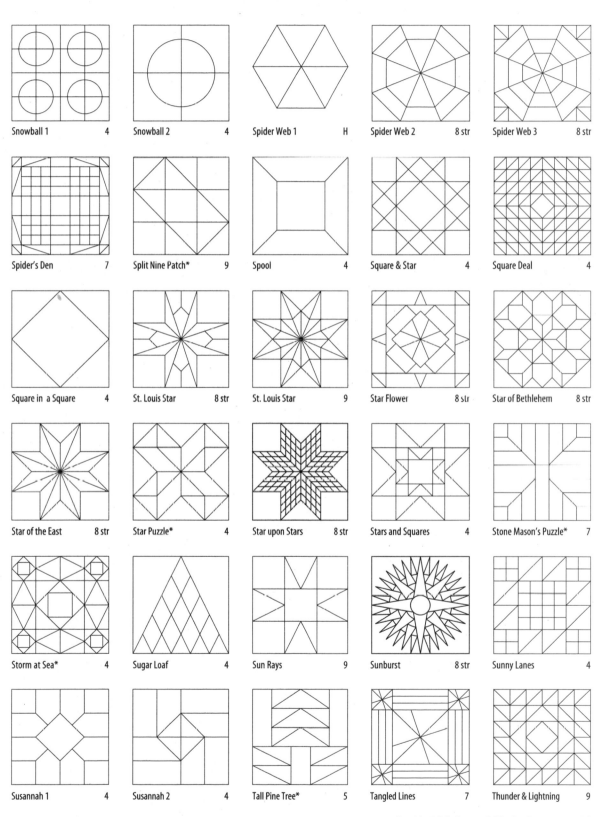

Snowball 1 4	Snowball 2 4	Spider Web 1 H	Spider Web 2 8 str	Spider Web 3 8 str
Spider's Den 7	Split Nine Patch* 9	Spool 4	Square & Star 4	Square Deal 4
Square in a Square 4	St. Louis Star 8 str	St. Louis Star 9	Star Flower 8 str	Star of Bethlehem 8 str
Star of the East 8 str	Star Puzzle* 4	Star upon Stars 8 str	Stars and Squares 4	Stone Mason's Puzzle* 7
Storm at Sea* 4	Sugar Loaf 4	Sun Rays 9	Sunburst 8 str	Sunny Lanes 4
Susannah 1 4	Susannah 2 4	Tall Pine Tree* 5	Tangled Lines 7	Thunder & Lightning 9

Visual Index
(number at right indicates the patch grid, asterisk indicates design is elsewhere in this book)

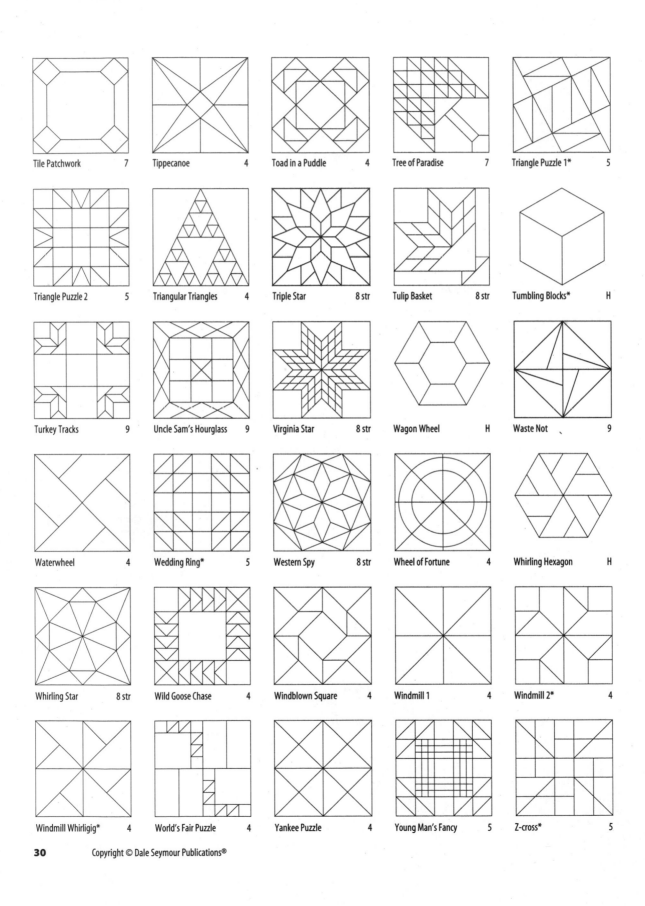

Tile Patchwork 7	Tippecanoe 4	Toad in a Puddle 4	Tree of Paradise 7	Triangle Puzzle 1* 5
Triangle Puzzle 2 5	Triangular Triangles 4	Triple Star 8 str	Tulip Basket 8 str	Tumbling Blocks* H
Turkey Tracks 9	Uncle Sam's Hourglass 9	Virginia Star 8 str	Wagon Wheel H	Waste Not 9
Waterwheel 4	Wedding Ring* 5	Western Spy 8 str	Wheel of Fortune 4	Whirling Hexagon H
Whirling Star 8 str	Wild Goose Chase 4	Windblown Square 4	Windmill 1 4	Windmill 2* 4
Windmill Whirligig* 4	World's Fair Puzzle 4	Yankee Puzzle 4	Young Man's Fancy 5	Z-cross* 5

3

Classic Symmetrical Designs

Eight-Pointed Star

Flying Swallows

Corn and Beans

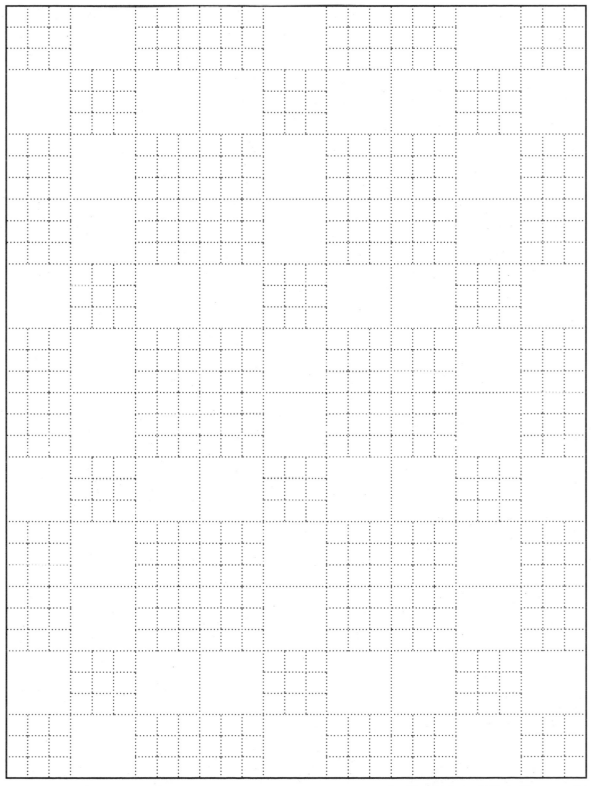

Stone Mason's Puzzle

Shoo Fly

Grandmother's Fan

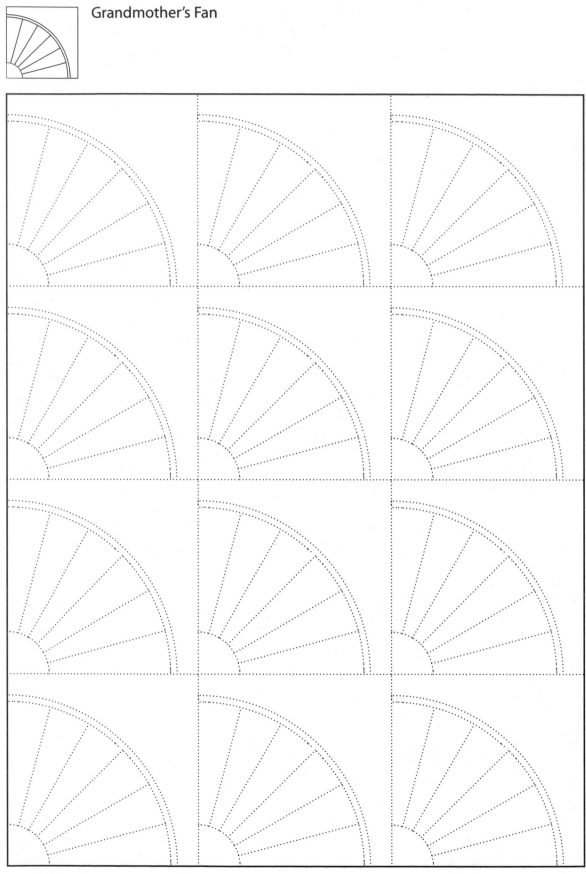

Farmer's Daughter

43

Windmill Whirligig

Star Puzzle

Storm at Sea

47

Tumbling Blocks

4

Designs with Variations

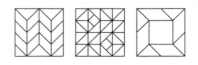

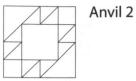 Anvil 2

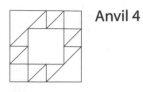 Anvil 4

Arabic Lattice 2

Arabic Lattice 4

Bachelor's Puzzle 2

Bachelor's Puzzle 4

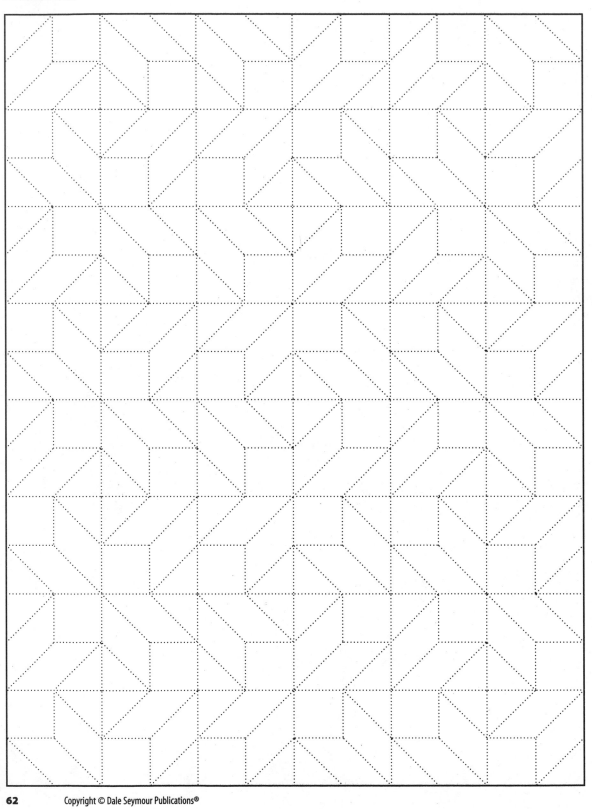

Box Quilt 2

Box Quilt 4

Chinese Puzzle 2

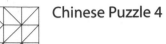 Chinese Puzzle 4

Chinese Puzzle 6

Churn Dash 1

73

Churn Dash 2

Churn Dash 4

Double Z 2

Dutchman's Puzzle 2

Dutchman's Puzzle 4

Flower Basket 2

Flower Basket 4

 Flower Basket 6

Hen and Chickens 2

Hen and Chickens 4

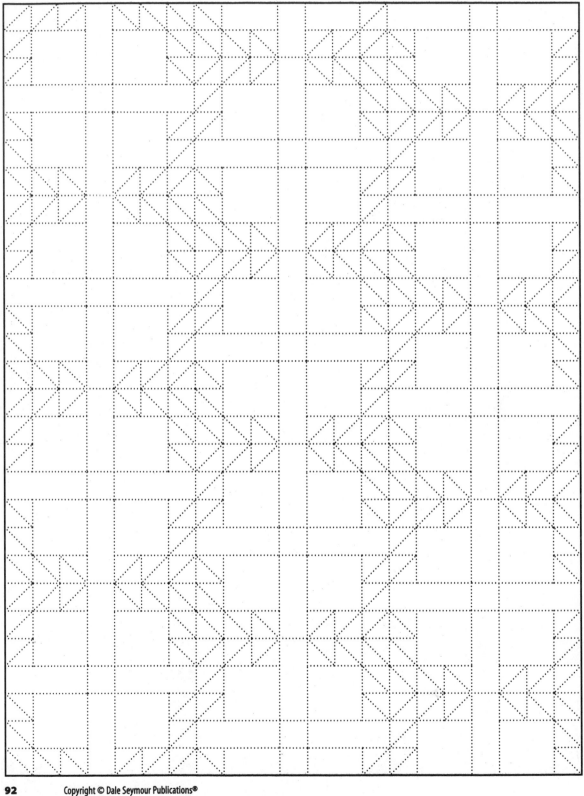

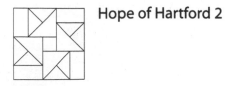 **Hope of Hartford 2**

Hope of Hartford 4

Jack-in-the-Box 2

Jack-in-the-Box 4

Lady of the Lake 2

Lady of the Lake 4

Next-Door Neighbor 2

Next-Door Neighbor 4

Nocturne 2

Nocturne 4

Old Maid's Puzzle 2

Old Maid's Puzzle 4

Road to Oklahoma 2

Road to Oklahoma 4

Shooting Star 2

Shooting Star 4

 Split Nine Patch 2

Split Nine Patch 4

Tall Pine Tree 2

Tall Pine Tree 4

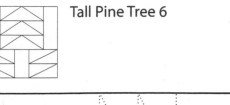

Tall Pine Tree 6

 Triangle Puzzle 2

Triangle Puzzle 3

137

Triangle Puzzle 4

Windmill 2

Windmill 3

Windmill 4

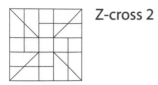 Z-cross 2

 Z-cross 4